PRAGUE WITH FINGERS OF RAIN

Vítězslav Nezval was published in the Penguin Modern European Poets series in *Three Czech Poets* (1971), a volume shared with Antonin Bartušek and Josef Hanzlík, translated by Ewald Osers and George Theiner. More recent translations of his work include *Antilyrik and Other Poems,* tr. Jerome Rothenberg & Miloš Sovak (Green Integer, 2001), *Edison*, tr. Ewald Osers (Dvořák, 2003), *Edition 69,* tr. Jed Slast (Twisted Spoon, 2004), *Valerie and Her Week of Wonders*, tr. David Short (Twisted Spoon, 2005), and *Prague with Fingers of Rain*, tr. Ewald Osers (Bloodaxe Books, 2009).

VÍTĚZSLAV NEZVAL
PRAGUE WITH FINGERS OF RAIN

TRANSLATED BY EWALD OSERS
FOREWORD BY IVAN KLÍMA

BLOODAXE BOOKS

ISBN: 978 1 85224 816 1

First published 2009 by
Bloodaxe Books Ltd,
Eastburn,
South Park,
Hexham,
Northumberland NE46 1BS.

www.bloodaxebooks.com

For further information about Bloodaxe titles
please visit our website and join our mailing list
or write to the above address for a catalogue.

Supported using public funding by

**ARTS COUNCIL
ENGLAND**

Cover design: Neil Astley & Pamela Robertson-Pearce.

This is a digital reprint of the Bloodaxe Books 2009 edition.

CONTENTS

ACKNOWLEDGEMENTS

Twenty-one of these translations were first published in *Three Czech Poets* (Penguin Books, 1971). Special thanks are due to Ivan Klíma for his foreword, which is first published here (in Ewald Osers' translation).

This translation has been subsidised by the Ministry of Culture of the Czech Republic

A remarkable member of the Avant-garde

Vítězslav Nezval, one of the greatest (but also most controversial) Czech poets, lived in a country whose history was rich in reversals and paradoxical changes, but also a country where poetry enjoyed extraordinary interest. Not only monthlies, but even the most serious Czech daily paper would carry a poem on their title pages. Some of the poets (even some rather bad ones) were considered national bards and every new collection they published became a social event. This was of course due to historical circumstances – it was the poets who became the main symbol of the national revival and the resurrection of the Czech language, and thus the birth of the modern Czech nation. The poetry of the 19th century was conservative and often didactic; one of its aims, repeatedly reiterated, was to prove that the Czech language was capable of expressing the most complex situations and that it was possible to translate into it the greatest works of world literature. Not until the end of the century did poetry begin to diversify and to reach artistic standards comparable to the poetry of the rest of Europe.

Almost symbolically, Nezval was born at the turn of the century – in the spring of 1900. He belonged to the exceptionally strong generation of poets that included the future laureate of the Nobel Prize, Jaroslav Seifert (one year younger than Nezval), and the gifted Jiří Wolker (who, however, died before he was able to develop his talent to the hights of his generational coevals). This generation also included the outstanding prose writer Vladislav Vančura (who was just under ten years older), as well as Karel Čapek, who was already internationally famous as a prose writer and playwright at a time when Nezval published his first poetry. Even though Karel Čapek never wrote poetry, he influenced the language of a whole generation by his superbly translated anthology of modern French poetry.

That generation was, while still young, marked by three historical upheavals – the First World War, the Bolshevik Revolution, followed by attempted revolutions in Europe, and finally by the emergence of an independent Czechoslovak Republic.

Nezval succeeded during the war in avoiding military service (though he lost several friends in the war); what influenced him much more at the time was the Bolshevik Revolution. Like most young poets he sympathised with it, he believed that socialism would do away with poverty and enable the socially weaker ones to lead a dignified life. In his first, youthfully naive (but formally astonishingly ripe and unconventional), poems we still encounter a social note or the belief that an Uprising is impending.

> People
> Look into each other's eyes
> Into the hearts
> No one above you
> All in a circle
> Holding hands
> All of you
> Each has his own mother country
> In your mother tongue
> Thunder forth
> All of you
> – Already we know
> This moment a world will rise from its swoon –
> It's breathing

At 24 he joined the Communist Party, but it seems that he was fascinated not so much by Lenin's utopian (and bloody) vision as by the Russian modern movement, which in the first years after the Revolution was for many artists identical with the idea of a poetry liberated from all constraints and bourgeois prejudices. Years later Nezval reminisced: 'To us the Soviet Union was an untouchable country... There, poetry had freed itself from trite symbolism, academism and tedious realistic miniature. We came to know the grand poetry of Mayakovsky and his friends... Even though we had been students on Montmartre and Montparnasse, none of us could truly regard himself as a "westerner", because the honest avant-garde in the West understood itself with the honest Soviet avant-garde...'

Although he declared himself for the Communist movement and also for the movement of revolutionary avant-garde artists in Czechoslovakia that called itself 'Devětsil', a group aiming at what they called 'proletarian art', Communist ideas gradually disappeared from Nezval's work. For a revolutionary he lacked one basic ability – the ability to hate and to write gloomily about a world that had not yet been "cleansed" by the proletarian revolution. Nezval was the very opposite – an essential optimist, a hedonist who enjoyed whatever life had in store for him. In a letter to a friend he admits: 'Teige, Vančura and a few of his friends have realised that we shall not be redeemed by the art of social hope, that the simple people are not asking social experience from us, and that proletarian art can be practised without official sentimentality... above all, that we do

10

not lack non-militancy or the courage to take off and fly cheerfully.'

One might say that an original and effective rhyme (never mind an evening in the company of friends or a pretty girl) was more important to Nezval than any revolutionary slogan.

Nezval was one of those exceptional creative persons for whom everything they encounter turns into poetry. The lightness of his verses is stunning (and at times dangerous to the poet himself: of his 85 titles by no means every one is superb). His ability to find countless metaphors for even the most everyday things was down-right extraordinary: his verses, whether free or rhymed, had a magical power of insinuating themselves into the reader's ear and engraving themselves indelibly in his memory. I recall how enchanted I was by the refrain in one of his best poems, 'Edison':

> But there was something beautiful to catch my breath
> Courage and pleasure over life and death

I have mentioned Čapek's anthology of translations from modern French poetry. It was, above all, his congenial translation of Apollinaire's *Zones* that influenced Nezval's first collections. He himself characterised his beginnings as follows: 'More than anything did we break and cut down forms, more than anything did we renounce forms, for repeated sentiments no longer captivated us; we raised the banner of an art that was able to utter everything for which the language of form had remained mute. I could now permit myself to make any theme the subject of my poetic interest and there was no danger that I would "develop" it the way the older poetry did. As when we water our garden with a watering can, a theme would become for me the subject of centrifugal rays.'

Later, on his frequent visits to Paris, he made the acqaintance of André Breton and became a passionate follower of surrealism.

That period (from which his poems about Prague date) may be regarded as the peak period of his creativity. Nezval had in him that which characterises a genius – the need forever to seek and find something new, a need further enhanced by the atmosphere of his day, which regarded novelty, freshness and rebellion against any tradition as its highest value, a period when artists like Picasso abandoned their style as soon as they had found it and hastened to find a new one. About surrealism Nezval recorded these personal remarks: 'Has not surrealism come to us just in time, has there not been a need for this moral and intellectual crisis in people who have passed thirty and who have so or so many courageous works behind them, and does not a man of thirty who has achieved this or that find himself on an inclined plane from which the way leads straight to resignation and betrayal...?'

It should be remembered that the avant-garde which he then avowed not only had a demonstratively positive attitude to the Soviet revolution, but also displayed a liking for manifestos and theoretical proclamations, though – fortunately – the creative writers were not greatly bothered with their requirements. Thus, Nezval's poems about Prague, which the English reader is offered here in Ewald Osers's fine translation, are not easily assigned to any school or movement. They are simply the original poems of an inspired poet at the peak of his creative powers.

For a country lad from Moravia, Prague, from the moment he first stood there, became a theme from which emanated 'centrifugal rays'. Prague between the two wars differed in many respects from the city today. From the but recently collapsed monarchy it retained both its bilinguality and its liking for cafés, wine-cellars and taverns, some of which became famous as the meeting places of writers and artists. Several dozen literary and art periodicals were published in Prague. Czech artists were at home there as much as German or Jewish ones (Franz Kafka was still alive, as was Max Brod, the streets of the city still bore the traces of its natives Werfel and Rilke), there were Czech and German secondary schools and universities, there was a Czech and a German theatre and the mutual contacts of the cultures had a significant influence on the creative environment. There was a lively night life as well as literary discussions. The avant-garde professed collectivism and the protagonists of its ideas were united by ties that were often unaffected by years or frontiers. The person with most influence on Nezval was probably his friend Karel Teige, one of the chief theoreticians of the avant-garde.

In that precipitate inter-war period avant-garde theories influenced all the arts. 'With contempt for bourgeois art,' Nezval recalled, 'and its psychologising filth and seeming glitter we let ourselves be guided by the correct goal, over to the roots, to the roots of man's inner life. That this was not to the liking of even some of our comrades...over that we didn't lose any sleep.'

On the eve of the Second World War, however, the 30-year-old, or nearly 40-year-old, poet again found himself on an inclined plane. Decisive for his decisions this time were not so much artistic manifestos as political events – above all, the criminal trials in Moscow. While most of his friends in the avant-garde refused to accept them, Nezval by then did not wish to get into conflict with 'the comrades'.

He preferred to part with his friends and his work until then. He left, or rather disbanded, the surrealist group he had helped to found.

The 'comrades' seized power in Czechoslovakia after the war, and the avant-garde – totally ignoring the appeals of the Soviet ideologists who demanded that art should serve the building of socialism, the proletariat and its class struggle, and who recognised socialist realism as the only movement – suddenly became the target of furious attacks. Nezval's friend Karel Teige was labelled 'the chief representative of the Trotskyite agency in Czech culture'. Some of Nezval's avant-garde friends committed suicide and Nezval himself, however loyally he behaved, was in danger.

Unlike Karel Teige, who refused to yield to the pressure (he died just a few days before he was due to be arrested), Nezval continued along the road he had chosen at the time of the Moscow trials. With the lightness typical of him he wrote a long servile poem in praise of one of the bloodiest tyrants in history, Stalin. Moreover, he added a prettily rhymed propaganda poem, 'Song of Peace', in which, at odds with his temperament, he cursed criminal imperialism in the spirit of Stalinist slogans.

By this unexpectedly degraded poetry he forged for himself a solid shield: none of the Party ideologists could any longer attack the man who had sung the praises of the ruling dictator and fighter for peace. For many admirers of Nezval his propaganda writings from the early 50s were not only a sign of the decline of his poetic powers, but also a stain on his entire oeuvre.

Nezval himself probably had no illusions about this work: for him his propagandist versifications were a tactical manoeuvre to preserve himself and the whole of his past work.

As the most highly acknowledged poet of the regime, honoured with the title 'National Artist', he could now do what no one else could: during the period of the Stalinist darkness he published his entire pre-war oeuvre. I remember to this day how, on that desert that had spread over the Czech book market and engulfed it with socialist-realist literary refuse, Nezval's pre-war poetry had the effect of living water, of an unexpected and unbelievable oasis. As soon as, following Stalin's death, the worst terror somewhat abated, Nezval did whatever he could to cleanse his dead or rejected friends and once more called for freedom for the artists as an indispensable prerequisite of creative work.

When he died in 1958 we printed in the periodical *Květen*, which the younger generation was allowed for a time to publish, not an obituary – which would have had to deal critically with the profound contrast between his pre-war and post-war work – but a poem that clearly revealed his real attitude to life:

> Lift off the burden of all heavy things
> Though destitute, walk with the step of kings
> Like cypress, moon and friend of dreams you'll try
> to raise the mighty sea up to the sky
>
> Let wings of bees your human injuries dress
> Fly without wings and rudderless
> Make light of human fate, count death for nothing
> and fly up to the heavens with your coffin!

IVAN KLIMA

PRAGUE WITH FINGERS OF RAIN

City of spires

Hundred-spired Prague
With the fingers of all saints
With the fingers of perjury
With the fingers of fire and hail
With the fingers of a musician
With the intoxicating fingers of women lying on their backs
With fingers touching the stars
On the abacus of night
With fingers from which evening gushes with tightly closed fingers
With fingers without nails
With fingers of the smallest children and pointed blades of grass
With the fingers of a cemetery in May
With the fingers of beggarwomen and the whole working class
With fingers of thunder and lightning
With fingers of autumn crocuses
With the fingers of the Castle and old women with harps
With fingers of gold
With fingers through which the blackbird and the storm whistle
With fingers of naval ports and dancing lessons
With the fingers of a mummy
With the fingers of the last days of Herculaneum and drowning
        Atlantis
With fingers of asparagus
With fingers of one-hundred-and-four-degree fevers
And frozen forests
With fingers without gloves
With fingers on which a bee has settled
With fingers of larch trees
With fingers cajoling a flageolet
In the night's orchestra
With the fingers of cardsharpers and pincushions
With fingers deformed by rheumatism
With fingers of strawberries
With the fingers of windmills and blossoming lilac
With fingers of mountain-springs with bamboo fingers
With fingers of clover and ancient monasteries
With fingers of french chalk
With fingers of cuckoos and Christmas trees
With the fingers of mediums

With admonishing fingers
With fingers brushed by a bird in flight
With the fingers of church bells and an old pigeon loft
With the fingers of the Inquisition
With fingers licked to test the wind
With the fingers of grave diggers
With the fingers of thieves of the rings
On hands telling the future
On hands playing the ocarina
With the fingers of chimney-sweeps and of St Loretto
With the fingers of rhododendrons and the water jet on the
        peacock's head
With the fingers of sinful women
With the sunburnt fingers of ripening barley and the Petřín
        Lookout Tower
With fingers of coral mornings
With fingers pointing upwards
With the cut-off fingers of rain and the Tyn Church on the glove
        of nightfall
With the fingers of the desecrated Host
With the fingers of inspiration
With long jointless fingers
With the fingers with which I am writing this poem

Walker in Prague

To climb and descend steps
Which lead nowhere
How often this nameless vertigo is conjured up

One day in April 1920 I arrived in Prague for the first time
At the station as sad as ashes huddled a dejected crowd
They were emigrants
And there I first saw the world I shall never understand
Midday was noisy but this was twilight and the station stretched
        far into the suburbs

You don't understand why they've shut you up in the morgue
Where you can smell boiled cabbage and the stench of the railway
The smell of my suitcase is making me cry
I shake like a pianola at the high notes
The yard hangs like an evil cloud outside the window from which
        I never lean
And everywhere I feel a stranger

Like a practical joke the Castle suddenly stands before me
I shut my eyes it was a mirage
A fragment of memory the tears are welling we are in Prague
I try in vain to sleep in the room where a man once shot himself

Thus I walked for days and nights on end
Unspeakably dejected
Everything was strange I did not dare to remember
Until one day
I met a memory
It was a friend
He took me along under his umbrella
We sat in a room the piano was playing at last I shall be able to
        love you Prague

Sitting on the embankment
It's past midnight we've come from a terrible cell
It was beautiful with a naked woman on a leather sofa
Under the water are strung garlands of lights
As if someone had folded an umbrella

Leaning over the Bridge of the Legions I shall watch this fiesta of
    parasols every day

It was difficult like the love of a woman from whom you are
    fleeing
The countless lodgings you changed in the course of your flight
Before you allowed her green eyes to trap you
Now in her footsteps the embankment changes into a terrace with
    Chinese lanterns
With the mayflies dying in the café windows
How often did you change your lodgings
Before you were bewitched by the ice-cream vendor in St Salvator
    Street

Thus I learned to love Prague
Thus I first heard the bird singing under an art-nouveau cornice
    of a shabby square
Thus the pain of your inconsolable sadness faded away
Thus in the sickly suburbs I found my Cinderella
Thus I became a walker in Prague
Thus I learned to have dates in your streets with adventure and love
Prague of my dreams

It is evening work has stopped the city is dancing
For your delight a thousand fans have opened
Your black coach is driving out from white houses
You'll be spinning round like a brilliant roundabout
The magnolia blossoms are bursting now they are dresses
They are dresses they are bonnets
They are your eyes they are your lips

Even on a rainy day she is radiant
She drops her roses I pick them up
She drops her roses everywhere even among the hideous laundry
    basements
My longing leads me about the city which seems to me as
    miraculous as a fountain playing over a cemetery
As a dragonfly over a sleeping woman as eyes in a lake
As a fire in a goldsmith's shop as a peacock on a belvedere
As a rainbow over a window where someone is playing the piano
As a comb from which sparks crackle on a bunch of carnations

As an umbrella with a hole burnt through by a meteor
As the fountain jet which you wave at me whenever I am sad
As Captain Corcoran's ship which has struck the Magnetic
       Mountain

St Wenceslas Square at evening

Sun-tanned girls
Like dark church corners
Indistinguishable from the wall
Which they form
Under the lamps in which the wind whistles

Good evening unknown lady
Dressed in the smells of the yawning street
How I adore you how I love you
One more day and we shall keep our illusions
Prague is blending with all other cities
As you blend with all women
Each having its own subtly different illusive perfume

The lilac by the museum on St Wenceslas Square

I don't love flowers
I love women
Yet I slept beneath the lilac
From afar came the breath of a cellar
Stuffy as main street apartments in the artificial night
Of your artificial eyes
Of your artificial lips
Of your artificial breasts and hair styles
I love you bunch of lilac
On the promenade where the gardens step out in the evening
With roses untold
Her breasts covered in rose petals
Prague breathes through open windows
Cool twilight
And while I was asleep
The lilac burst into flower on St Wenceslas Square

Four p.m. on a certain day in spring

I read a story
I forget its title
All I remember is a wooden table
In the yard
A nameless town and holidays
Today it came back to me
On the café terrace
Coal carts are rumbling past
In a strawberry forest, an overturned jug
My mother's voice not calling me for afternoon cake
Women trailing the fragrant smoke of English cigarettes
It is always I
The boy from the forgotten story
Intently watching
The tourniquet set alight by the sun's last ray

The Jewish Cemetery

On 21 November 1921
I was walking down from the Petřín Viewing Tower
When suddenly the sunset
Severed me from my past

I stopped
Surprised by the hours that were extinguished in the tree tops

Then a mist fell

I walked with my collar turned up
I walked avoiding the streets that fascinate me
I walked until the wind which mixed the headlights
Caused me to stop in a half-wrecked thoroughfare

From the façade opposite above the second-hand shop
Boxes flew out whirling up the dust
I caught sight of a date
Whose numbers began to rearrange themselves
Also I thought that I was seized by vertigo

I took out a cigarette
Glad that the wind had dropped
And got ready to move on
When the numerals by some unknown caprice
Still on the wall formed my date of birth

I wanted to cry out for help and shut my eyes
And from my throat against my will escaped a faint moaning
That might as well have come from someone else
But it alarmed me
I remained frozen in the door
Which suddenly flew open with a gust

I found myself in a room
In a novel somewhere on its final pages
On a chaise longue
The sofa's springs creaked
I wrapped her into a cloak

For a long time she couldn't part from her charming foot
Not even when she got up straightening her hair and dress
When from a stringbag at her waist she took out a little stone
And through the half-open window let me look
Into a strange mixture of stones and trees which I couldn't tell apart

Then I saw her climbing over the low cemetery wall
From the long row of little stones in front of a tomb
She picked one up and burst out laughing
She put it into her bag revealing her legs with which she'd made
      love to me

Gripped by fury
I throttled her
I throttled her until
Her eyes had lost all sparkle

Then I walked home
In a fever
From which I awoke in some unfamiliar house
Without people

Then I went mad

I don't know how much later
I was awakened by three knocks at the door

It was morning
I rose from my bed
By my library over which hung several photographs
The woman I love stepped up to me
With a smile as at every other meeting
She stroked my face
She didn't stop smiling
And turned my desperation into terror
I was also looking for that stone I'd been given
So she should believe me
To my horror I produced from my pocket a piece of gold
I looked at my watch
It was lunchtime

We hurried to yesterday's brothel which suddenly wasn't there
I saw before me a walled-up house
The date was hidden by the pigeons' wings
And where yesterday a second-hand shop was
Stood now a catafalque with an open coffin

Lying in it was an old woman with open eyes
I recognised those precious old eyes full of light
I recognised those precious dead eyes without light
They told me she was the last woman who understood astrology
They took her to the Jewish cemetery
And on her tomb I placed a golden stone
Without gold

Later I asked the historians the meaning of the date that had
        terrified me
It was the day of the alchemist's death
It was the date of my birth
I collect the little stones you threw at me
My friends and you the future cities I never visited
Wonderful women I throttled
Chimeras I sacrificed all my time to
They'll turn into inalienable jewels
That betray my alchemy

The bells of Prague

The bells of Prague are waving to you to leave your cupboards
The bells of Prague are waving to you to step down into the streets
Where I wander in search of a girl
The bells of Prague are tolling out your funeral
In my heart which now expects nothing
The bells of Prague are guiding me past baited traps
The bells of Prague are calling all of you
Whom I have held in my arms without even knowing your names
The bells of Prague are calling all the cats' eyes that ever followed
    me over the threshold
Past the same smirking blind hunchback
The bells of Prague are calling all my friends
The bells of Prague are calling all my memories
The bells of Prague are calling the days when death was no evil
The bells of Prague are calling all the fists
All fists to hammer against miraculous window-panes
The bells of Prague are calling all the nuns
To show their white
Love-denying knees
The bells of Prague are calling all whores
Under whose window sleepwalkers pass
The bells of Prague are calling all the children
All children to utter together their Why
Over a star or a nightingale
Over something frightening that looks like a featherbed
The bells of Prague are calling all crazy melancholics
The bells of Prague are calling all the stars shed by a yearning night

Women washing windows

You made a date with a poem
In the pub garden where you're writing and looking up
That poem is a pair of legs like the tongue of a bell
Under a skirt with which the wind is playing
And which waves to you
To drop everything
And climb the stairs to that beautiful exhibitionist
To breed with her before the eyes of the whole street
To breed her and yourself
With the eternal longing to breed miraculous women with
           miraculous thighs
With a miraculous ability to open their womb
In any window of any street

Strangers' faces

Some day when men understand your poetry city that I come to
         on the road
Where the signposts read Fidelity
There will no longer be the strangers' faces
That have come
Today
To scare my sorrow to scare the spring
They will not be like the loveless embrace
In which an unforgivable chill
Begot them
They will not be like their ill-built houses
Of ambition
And greed
They will not be stale
As their thoughts as their dreams
As their theatre performances
As the beer in which they drown their indifference
As stars seen over paper blinds
They will be like balconies
Like the roses of Prague
Rapturous as the river
Sweeter than the chimes of St Loretto
O for an age to put an end to all this tastelessness
That makes Prague a crowd jostling for cigarettes
That makes me prefer the conversation of tower clocks to that of
         people
And then a foreign visitor will come
To bow to the women of Prague
Who will no longer be embarrassed
Who will no longer be ashamed of the sweet name of Prague
And poetry will raise its lamp amidst the woods

Museum

The hot summer afternoons
Make me think of a day
       when I will be able to continue without interruption
If you too wish to enjoy this illusion today
Come with me for a while to the Museum

Wilson railway station

There's been no letter and no telegram
Adventure's playing blind-man's-buff with you
If you stand on the platform someone will arrive you can be sure
        of that
The two of you will carry the luggage or else you'll follow them
        as the third man

St Nicholas's Church

When I'm wearing my green beret and the sun is setting
I look at St Nicholas's Church
Its dome also has an eccentric colour and it doesn't think
Mischievous sparrows give my head a miss

The clock in the old Jewish ghetto

While time is running away on Příkopy Street
Like a racing cyclist who thinks he can overtake death's machine
You are like the clock in the ghetto whose hands go backwards
If death surprised me I would die a six-year-old boy

Balconies

Remember friend that you are neither fish nor bird
You sought an embrace and you found balconies
Man sometimes holds up his head Oh what vertigo
It is never too late for a party
Among the baroque lamps or trellis work cages

At last you've learned to light the Chinese lanterns
To see white beauties in the preachers' pulpits
They step out wearing golden slippers
With coloured tassels waving from their elbows
They are tiny china cups raised to toast the city

I know a house
Tall as a coiffure a cockade or a rose
A house with breasts adorned with garlands
The breasts are bared to the little golden cross
They kneel like processions

At midnight the balcony is a widow
Playing a game of chess with someone above the city
She's standing naked lamp in hand
A nightmare comes to her like a pocket mirror
A key tinkles against the pavement
A bud falling someone has scattered a handful of diamonds
The balcony rises up like an empty dress
The wind fills its empty glove with jasmine perfume

You're looking at the hanging baskets
With a torch flaming above them
Coronets sitting easily on any head
A shooting star
As in a blazing house
The meeting of woman and fire
You see the unequal struggle
Of fiery hand with burning flame

How beautiful are the balconies in a century of breastless women
Among houses humming with life
They are beautiful like a fountain playing for a funeral

Like a womb from which emerges the head of spring
Of flower-strewn skyless couches

I walk past those black and white washstands
Over which hangs a haze
As if someone said goodnight
As if someone breathed a sigh
As if someone spoke to me softly
Oh balconies

Doves of marble from divans
Ever ready to rise flapping their wings
In the full moon's light they are frozen shoulders
Covered with a shower of confetti
But this afternoon
They are even more beautiful they are glass cases
In vain do you look for the woman whose scent has sent you to
      sleep

As if a wedding procession had just passed
Oh gondolas
As if I were picking up a lost handkerchief
As if somewhere a lily-of-the-valley were fading away
Black swans and white swans prepare to fly away above the closed
      windows

One more glance
One more chord
One more beat of wings in the red light of evening
And the houses will start moving house
Someone is playing a guitar
Someone is saying goodbye or flinging a bunch of flowers

When

When the Charles Bridge is overgrown with grass
Come with me love to chase the geese away

When Prague will be in the woods
I'll fall in love with a wood nymph

When a nightingale sings in Tyn Church
Come listen to it leave excuses at home

When the Three Kings come straight out of prison
All bells will ring as they are ringing today

When embroidered trees grow on balconies
A shepherd will be piping his tune there

When you'll put a thunderstorm or at least lightning into your
        hat band
It will be the end of the world or perhaps just its beginning

The suburb

The suburb is a bright straw hat
With an unfinished card game
The suburb is a removal van
Everything's in it chairs and wickerwork
The buildings are badly wrapped cheese
And also a cheap cloth cap
The suburb is smoking like a youth with a tatty whodunnit

Covered market

Enchanting girl your breasts are playing with the morning sun
They thrust upwards
They are sisters to bunches of grapes and unmoored airships
Meanwhile her kitchen forgotten she walks on the ground

The pavement vibrates
Whenever her sandal
Like sage
Dances under the flowery garland of the dubious twilight
Like a bunch of schoolgirls hurrying to their lessons

With lilies-of-the-valley fading in their nostrils they enter the morgue
Turkeys are hanging there rabbits and disobedient young goats
Still swinging from their gallows
There are vats of blood
Stylishly like an executioner a woman peels off her glove
Her hair-do trembles
Like some dreadful paper
A pheasant stares with desperate eyes
The market mixes its colours like a painter
Under its railway-station vault they meet behind the backs of
        fattened calves

Gone are the men gone is their tyranny
This is the woman's realm
Here no questions are asked
Beautiful fingers are plunged in a tub where fish swim
Here you haggle with no embarrassment
I feel as if I had stepped into a spectral dance-hall

Men don't know
What's happening in the world when they're locked away in their
        offices
They don't know the colour of a quail
They don't know the world born out of eggs
I want to try the weight of a brace of partridges
I feel as though I'm sleeping in a giant cage
The eyes of the birds hypnotise that woman with her vacant stare
This is like a cemetery on All Souls' Day

The clock strikes
Confusion grows the dissecting lab is tidied up
Quite soon the market will be as deserted as the world after the flood
There will be deep silence
And the smell of entrails
The women are leaving
Leaving grumpily

The sun plays with the billiard balls
And with the brilliant plumage in the brilliant bag
Their shopping done the women go and sniff the lilac
Their shopping done the women go and put on fresh lipstick
Garish as a Chinese lantern feast in the covered market

Panorama of Prague

Like berets hurled into the air
Berets of boys, cocottes and cardinals
Turned into stone by the sorcerer Žito
At the great feast
Berets with Chinese lanterns
On the eve of St John's Day
When fireworks go up
Yet also like a town of umbrellas opened skyward as a shield
       against rockets
All this is Prague

Leaning over a wall
I want to break this twig of wonderful blossoms

My eyes drink in the lights of the great merry-go-round
Whose ringing chimes call home
All its barges and stray horses
Whose ringing chimes call home
All sparks of light

Old Prague in the rain

Old City rains
A harp
From the Castle flies a wind-tattered rag
That melancholy flag
Waving goodbye from century to century
To the sun which buries a distant ocean
The flag loyal to eternal sorrow
Far too long has the nation wept under it
The harp twangs
Gloomy prophecies and coal-black birds settling on the palaces
In mourning windows a crimson torch is lit and doused
The drummer has stretched the drumskin and waits for the
            execution to start
Old women lock themselves m their homes
A burst of noise
A dreadful ceremony for the dead
Rosaries click between the fingers of old women and spires
They are spilled like hailstones rattling against coffins

In the square the funeral pomp has all been left behind
It's raining
The voice of the clocks
The voice of the knell
A procession of black umbrellas
The mourning women have a vision of a phantom horseman

Obscure hotels

An ageless gentleman
With light luggage
Steps into
A cupboard
In a rainy street
Out of which stepped
An ageless lady
Without luggage
Into the muddy day
They've never met
And never will meet
Only the washstand
Which she didn't empty
And the cigar
Which he threw away
Will remind them
Outside another hotel
Which she has entered
Arid he has left
That they have known each other
For the best part of a year
And so one day
The ageless gentleman
With the luggageless lady
Will step into
A cupboard
In a rainy street
Where there, are
Curtains
A washstand
And a single coat hook

The Little City Square

A knight-errant
With at iron gauntlet
Knocks on the door
Of the Little City Square palaces
No one opens to him
He's got the wrong door
He's got the wrong century
The last tavern is closing
He recognises the voice of the clock
Its deep sound
He is hungry
He should be at home
Somewhere indoors
His bed is probably untouched
He's had a drop too much
Like the watchman
Who does not answer
Once more he knocks
At the wall
And falls asleep
Propped up against the façade
Along which I am walking home
As drowsy as that iron man

Night of acacias

Life has two or three days of love: then this withered tree hangs
     full of a thousand bees and blossoms
Like the one night in June when the acacias bloom and die
The river wears a chaplet of lights and is fragrant with embalmed
     bathers
The streets are suddenly wide and sparkling like beauty parlours
From beyond the river over hanging budges with rosaries of lights
Invisible gardens are on the march colliding with walkers
They're off to their rendezvous with the parks and the alleys of
     the central squares and main streets
Benumbed I do not recognise the old streets of the New City
Whose plain and graceless walls are today majestic as palace courts
O night of acacias of mountains and of that treacherous pianissimo
     stay
Make me for ever yearn for love and for Prague
O night at the end of June short-lived as passionate love as sensual
     delight
O night of acacias do not pass before I have crossed all the bridges
     of Prague
In my search for no one not a friend not a woman not even myself

O night with summer in your wake I long to breathe unendingly
     your raven hair
Your diamonds have bewitched me I want to look for them in the
     waters poor fisherman that I am
Oh if at least I could say au revoir to you
O night in June
If I were never to see you agam
Let me dissolve in your embrace my evil fate my love

Chimneys

The barrels of the chimneys are bombarding the blue skies
The flames of the machine-guns join in with their rattle
On every rooftop three and three
By tomorrow the banner will turn to a black flag of mourning
The pigeon turns black the raven turns grey
Those gun-barrels of the chimneys are terrible
But it would be still more terrible if they stopped their bombardment
Of the clouds over the city
For that would mean that they had run out of ammunition
The swallow would return
You'd feel the distant mountain air blowing down
And men would fall in the streets
With shirts as white as their faces
The red flags will no longer turn black overnight
There'll be so many of them
That the birds will flock round them
And the people march under them as under a red morning sky
The barrels of the chimneys will thunder out again
The machine-guns will start ticking
The bells will crash down from the towers
But instead of the knell will come the notes of retreat announcing
The coming of the age of love without smoke without chimneys

The Powder Tower

Evening is falling behind the Powder Tower
D'you see that long procession
It's a coronation retinue or a hearse
Or anyway umbrellas with a trail
Longer than advent
You feel as if past centuries were striding
To the pillory or into the museum
As if they were carrying someone on a tumbrel
As if some aggressive gang were chasing down the street
As if some carnival bells were dancing along
Here's a removal van
A plague ambulance
The horses observing the ceremonial
Women turning into trails
Men marching menacingly
A dog baring its teeth in fright
As before a storm
As before a solar eclipse
As if someone had suddenly died
As if a criminal was hiding here
Night
A widow in mourning
Walks with a lamp in her hand
Through the window blown out by the wind
Into infinite darkness
At its end shines the city

Rabbi Löw

You looked for poetry and found a legend
At last the stories about Rabbi Löw are of some use
It is your incident, poetry
It is your incident as if I didn't know you yet you're holding out
        your hand across the centuries
It was you who crossed the stone bridge to get an audience of the
        emperor
The mob greets you with stones but your clothes are pelted not
        with mud but with flowers
Your house differs from all other homes
You are a lion and also a bunch of grapes
You give life to things of clay and from it create dogged creatures
Into their mouths you place a *shem*
His power lasts for centuries or for a week
Every Friday it needs renewing
And yet, poetry, why did you kill the Golem
It's terrible to have the mysterious writing wiped off your forehead
To be carried up into the attic and turn to dust
Enviously you lie in wait for death to take from its hand some
        letters
Where your name is listed among those destined to die
This time you have escaped but ultimately, poetry, you'll find
Death hidden in the rose

Prague in winter

You're struggling with the wind the bells are silent the city has
    built a snowman
On Petřín Hill where women aimlessly wander with eyes of Snow
    White
The river flows as if someone were striking an anvil
Like a postal van with a mailbag burst open
The roofs like crows can't move a wing
The whistle freezes like a bird like a stick of sugar-candy
The spires are haughty wearing their ballroom gloves
The night weeps while it decorates the Christmas tree
Instead of people all you see is puppets and rabbitskin rags
Instead of people all you see is hate frozen to foreheads
Lips from which bushes grow
Eyes with a purplish glare of arc-lights
Under lamps like ostrich eggs
Under lamps lined up like an army on ceremonial parade
An army of deaf-mutes
As if there were no point in speaking
As if there were nothing to say
As if Prague were lost in an alien universe

Office girls

At half past seven on Monday morning Mary stands under an
        umbrella waiting for a tram
Bertha has just had her second shower
Anne's fastener has torn off she's waving at the driver smiling
The car is crowded they probably won't find a seat
When they stand close to each other it's like a guelder rose blooming
Their charms are puffed up like a doughnut with cream
Through their eyes the Sunday evening looks at the world
Through their eyes the Sunday morning looks at the world when
        you can go out into the woods
Through their eyes the cursed children look at the world
Hermina that pain in the arse is getting married
The tram stops the processions are multiplying
The processions
What tune is the pretty typist playing on her keys
She's reading a book she's reading it from the end
When I meet them in the evening it'll be no longer them but a
        few dusty bunches of flowers

Encounter

I met my adolescence in an old man's eyes
He was going for a walk as he did years ago
In a small country town
It was lovely there
And hidden somewhere there was today's day

You feel as if you had to sit your exam again
You don't go to school you've refused to write an article
You read the titles of the books in the shop-window
You drift about write poems as a student
You're looking for a woman with the evil eye

I feel like saying goodbye to you, Prague
Prague, my precious ring
A hundred times your emerald has fascinated me
A long time we didn't understand each other
Leaning over the bridge I greet the white sailing boats
I feel a little lonely I feel like you
I think I'll never meet you here again
I see them as a beautiful rime-covered bunch of grapes

You're sad
You smoke your first cigarette
And out loud memorise Homer
You should also learn to work with logarithms
Again you are madly in love
It is a woman with the head of a black marguerite
It is a woman with the lips of scales and midnight
It is a woman with the breasts of a cup and the moon
You wait for her each day in the beggarwomen's quarter
You wait for her each day she'll never come again

In the forest
Is the place
Where the snake took off its crown
The novel ends
Like the sun that's setting behind Petřín Hill
Leaving behind a vague little song
The river repeats it a hundred times a day
The bargee waves his handkerchief at a bird

You'll be observing Venus
Although no telescope has seduced me to do so
No hurdy-gurdy and no street astronomer
It is your more than thirty-year-old star
It is a finger incessantly tapping at fate
It is the full stop after a day that robbed you of everything
It is the down from the featherbed of women who have left
It is a whistle blown by a rose
It is the eye of earliest memories
It is the end of time it is a golden compass
It is the most faithful lamp of the evening
It is love that you don't know the end of

No longer do I want you to swear to me
No longer do I need to swear to you
Learn from now on to walk in the street
Learn from now on to play the organ
That is Prague
No prettier and no uglier than you
No prettier and no uglier than other women than other cities

Christmas shop-windows

There are eyes like long winter days when dusk starts falling in
        the morning
There are windows like mirages
You have nothing in there is everything
It is like your imagination
It is like a long dormant volcano that has finally thrown away its
        pipe
It is like the most scorching summer you can imagine
The shore ends here you are allowed no further
It is like an oasis within arm's reach and yet so infinitely far away
Snow is falling
Artificial suns are burning gold and luxury
It's snowing in the happy midnight isles
There's everything here that makes a woman beautiful and a man
        proud
There's everything here that gives a child a taste of infinity
A wondrous light mocks the powerless sun like a cold fireplace
        and a snowflake
There's everything there and everything is deceptive
You stand like a thief of fire who mustn't snatch even a ray

Deserted Sunday

One Sunday I strayed to a cemetery
I didn't know
A cemetery in a parched suburb
It was Žižkov
I was encountering women
They nodded to me
With eyes as closed as barber's shops
I also caught sight of a few bright neckties
Which I love
As I do bright women in forests
A few young workers were standing outside the cinema
After that I encountered no one

And yet
Paris and its seventeenth district
As if I were walking past the Lariboisière hospital
A restaurant
And a Russian band
I was hoping to meet a woman
As I do now
Lost in Prague not far from where I live

Hotels are beautiful
Without guests
An empty bar empty rooms
            in the middle of an empty city
As if I were a child whose parents had gone away
As if I'd been left alone
In a room that no one enters
As if you'd suddenly arrived on horseback
From the nearby castle
Where there's a swan
As if I were to meet you
Outside the hotel that no one goes to
Why do I see somewhere in a happy region
A villa in the middle of Sunday
Why do you disappear inside it
Why do I hear singing accompanied by a piano

I stepped into the wine-bar
Without people
To tremble later at your knees
On the Můstek
Prague of our secrets
A bird is singing in St Wenceslas Square
It's your deserted Sunday

Moon over Prague

The decorator is mixing his plaster
He's lit an oil-lamp on top of the stepladder
It is the moon
It moves like an acrobat
Wherever it appears it causes panic
It turns black coffee into white
It offers paste jewellery to women's eyes
It changes bedrooms into death chambers
It settles on the piano
It floodlights the Castle theatrically
Today Prague remembers its history
It's the river fête look at that bobbing Chinese lantern
The bells are as brittle as plates
There'll be a grand tourney
White carpets are laid throughout the city
Buildings have their roles in the great tragedy and all belongs to
       the underworld
The moon enters the tiny garrets
It gleams on the table it is an inkwell
A thousand letters will be written with its ink
And a single poem

Book City

1

There are mysterious cities and books bound in leather
Like naked women in forests
Like mulatto women with silver tattoos
Like water nymphs on subterranean paths
Like encounters between the eyes of wild pansies and men
Like preserved red currant in the beak of a storm
Like periwinkle valleys with the song of shepherds
Like flakes of snow and wild geese
Like anger of the womb
Like the touch of the fingers of night and burdock
I love them and forever seek them as I seek you, Prague, in your
      libraries exposed to the rain

2

There are days when the book city pursues me
I'd like to describe it
It is a book bound in green leather
Like naked women in forests
A book that's a nocturnal moth
Or a book that's a lake
It surrenders to my hands
Like a centifolia rose
It phosphoresces in the night
Like Prague under the full moon

Prague in the midday sun

I have not woken from a dream nor arrived by express train
I am spared the bother of seeing the sights like a tourist
For years I have not opened a book of fairytales
I don't expect love to reveal the universe or even this world
I don't want to sing with the birds nor rave about undersea
      landscapes
I've no illusions about nations which rule the world or about
      foreign settlements
I don't regard the people whose language I speak as either better
      or worse than those of other countries
I'm linked with the fate of the world's disasters and only have a
      little freedom to live or die

It is late in the morning
I am sitting under a coloured parasol – Prague lies down there
After long rains an amethyst vapour is rising
I see her through the filigree of trees as a maniac sees his phantasm
I see her as a great ship whose mast is the Castle
Like the enchanted cities of my visions
Like the great ship of the Golden Corsair
Like the dream of delirious architects
Like the throned residence of Magic
Like Saturn's palace with its gates flung open to the sun
Like a volcano fortress hewn by a raving madman
Like a guide to solitary inspiration
Like an awakened volcano
Like a bracelet dangling before mirrors

It is noon
Prague is sleeping and yet awake like a fantastic dragon
A sacred rhinoceros whose cage is the sky
A stalactite organ playing softly
A symbol of resurrection and of treasures of dried-up lakes
An army in panoply saluting the emperor
An army in panoply saluting the sun
An army in panoply turned into jasper

Magic city I have been gazing too long at you with blind eyes
Looking for you in the distance oh today I know it
You are obscure as the fires deep in the rocks as my fantasy
Your beauty has sprung from caverns and subterranean agates
You are old as the prairies over which song spreads its wings
When your tower clocks strike you are opaque as an island night
Exalted as the tombs as the crowns of Ethiopian kings
As if from a different world a mirror of my imagery
Beautiful as the mystery of love and improbable clouds
Beautiful as the mystery of speech and primordial memory
Beautiful as an erratic block marked by the rains
Beautiful as the mystery of sleep of stars and of phosphoresence
Beautiful as the mystery of thunder of the magic lamp and of poetry

If ever, Prague, you are in danger...

Fuel tanks are filling up and somewhere a bumblebee
Buzzes in a cloud above Prague as it prepares for supper
In this organ swell and the sighing bushy treetops of smacking
       tongues every sound is lost
Only the hearts of those in love and the sentries spot the nettle in
       the constellation of Orion

Like a hand seared by lightning
That drunken giant imitating a bird shudders
Like an apocalyptic beak flown up to peck out something
But also like a plumbline aiming downwards and suddenly falling
To tear off a piece of roof to burn out dearest agate eyes

If ever, Prague, you are in danger if your blacked-out windows
Are wrenched from their hinges by a hurricane and meteors come
       crashing down
To crown you with fire to burst into the sleep of your churches
To espouse the scattered rosary of your pomegranates
May your towers turn into cannon and fight back with golden swords
But if this, my city, if this were to happen
You must not act the wealthy lady who casts her ring to the river
The heartless lady accursed by the beggar's clairvoyant eyes
Or else the fish's oracle will haunt you and forever
You'd have to go a-begging   Yes forever
My faithless beauty my love

Prague with fingers of rain

It is not in anything
Not in anything that can be explained in terms of beauty or style
It is not the Powder Gate nor the Old City Square nor Charles
        Bridge
Neither old nor new Prague
It is not in anything that can be pulled down and not in anything
        that can be built up again
It is not in your legends Prague nor in your beauty
That you are unique in this world that you cannot change even if
        they destroy you
Your poetry is complex and I puzzle it out
As we divine the thoughts of beloved women
One cannot describe you one cannot draw you one cannot hold up
        a mirror to you
I would not recognise you any more than you would recognise
        yourself

It is not in anything
Not in anything that can be uttered by a glib tongue that can be
        described in a tourist guide
It is in your whole being in its mysterious disposition
In how a bird perches on your forehead
In how a child calls out to his mother as they walk past a baroque
        statue
In how a cyclist rides down the street while someone is singing
In the smell of the tramcars while the bells of St Loretto ring out
In how a tatty elegance is reflected in the windows of your
        warehouses and churches
In how a frankfurter tastes in the vaults which date back to the
        Thirty Years' War
In how intense the Czech language sounds in a deserted square
In how we haggle over the price in a record shop
In how you are dead on the picture postcards when the postman
        rings
In how dress shop assistants measure fat women who bear the
        names of your streets
In how a ham glistens as the sun sets behind Petřín Hill
I'm one of those men and women I love but who revolt me
Better only in wanting nothing and at times speaking honestly

And in having a passion for the infinite and in seeking that passion
        in you

Daughter of this afternoon and of remotest centuries
I don't want anything I am only a tongue
Your tongue your squeezed accordion
I am the tongue of your bells but also of your rain
I am the tongue of your grapes but also of your doss-houses
I am the tongue of your desiccated nuns but also of your drivers
I am the tongue of your slovenliness but also of your melancholia
I am the tongue of your swimming races but also of your primary
        schools
I am the tongue of your waiters but also of your influenza
I am the tongue of your roses but also of your cooked meats
I am the tongue of your wicker chairs but also of your weddings
I am the tongue of your grass but also of your bells
I am the tongue of your snack bars but also of your piano teachers
I am the tongue of your Sunday boredom but also of your weirs
I am the tongue of your fire siren but also your legends
I am only your tongue come to life
What leave-taking
When I want to go on listening to you even in my dreams
For you to appear to me as I have known you a hundred times as
        I have never known you before
For you to appear to me as if for the first time

To future generations I bequeath my experience and a long sigh
For the unfinished song which wakes me which lulls me to sleep
Remember me
That I lived and walked about Prague
That I learned to love her in a way no one loved her before
That I learned to love her like a son like a stranger
That I learned to love her with the free heart of a fancy-free man
        with free dreams and desires
That I learned to love her like a man who owns the future
That I learned to love her as no one loved her before
As her son and as a stranger
Cry and laugh set all your church bells ringing
As I have tried to set all the bells of memory ringing
For time flies and there's so much left I want to say about you
Time flies and I have still not said enough about you
Time flies like a swallow lighting up the old stars over Prague

Printed in the USA
CPSIA information can be obtained
at www.ICGtesting.com
JSHW021511200224
57736JS00001B/163